Modern Art
for Kids

Modern Art for Kids

Hands-On Art and Craft Activities Inspired by the Masters

Stephanie Ho Poon

Illustrated by Shannon Yeung

ROCKPORT

Inspiring | Educating | Creating | Entertaining

Brimming with creative inspiration, how-to projects, and useful information to enrich your everyday life, quarto.com is a favorite destination for those pursuing their interests and passions.

First Published in 2023 by Quarry Books, an imprint of The Quarto Group,
100 Cummings Center, Suite 265-D, Beverly, MA 01915, USA.
T (978) 282-9590 F (978) 283-2742 Quarto.com

Quarry Books titles are also available at discount for retail, wholesale, promotional, and bulk purchase. For details, contact the Special Sales Manager by email at specialsales@quarto.com or by mail at The Quarto Group, Attn: Special Sales Manager, 100 Cummings Center, Suite 265-D, Beverly, MA 01915, USA.

10 9 8 7 6 5 4 3 2

ISBN: 978-0-7603-8207-3

Digital edition published in 2023
eISBN: 978-0-7603-8208-0

Library of Congress Cataloging-in-Publication Data

Names: Ho Poon, Stephanie, author. | Yeung, Shannon, illustrator.
Title: Modern art for kids : hands-on art and craft activities inspired by
   the masters / Stephanie Ho Poon ; illustrated by Shannon Yeung.
Description: Beverly, MA : Rockport, 2023. | Includes index. | Audience:
   Ages 6-10 | Summary: "From Monet and Matisse to Van Gogh and Warhol,
   Modern Art for Kids is a guide to 20+ renowned artists, designed for
   both adults and children to enjoy together"-- Provided by publisher.
Identifiers: LCCN 2022054915 (print) | LCCN 2022054916 (ebook) | ISBN
   9780760382073 (paperback) | ISBN 9780760382080 (ebook)
Subjects: LCSH: Handicraft--Juvenile literature. | Art, Modern--Juvenile
   literature. | Art movements--Juvenile literature.
Classification: LCC TT160 .P66 2023 (print) | LCC TT160 (ebook) | DDC
   745.5083--dc23/eng/20221117
LC record available at https://lccn.loc.gov/2022054915
LC ebook record available at https://lccn.loc.gov/2022054916

Photography: Monika Kulon-Winspear and Shutterstock for picture frames
Illustration: Shannon Yeung

Printed in China

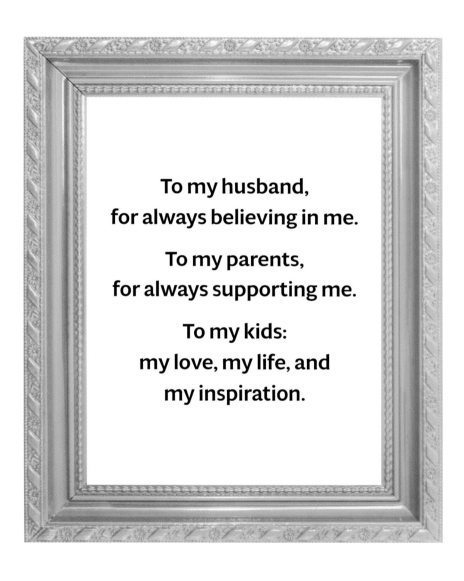

To my husband,
for always believing in me.

To my parents,
for always supporting me.

To my kids:
my love, my life, and
my inspiration.

CONTENTS

FRIDA KAHLO

VINCENT VAN GOGH

ABOUT THIS BOOK

For thousands of years, people have been making and enjoying art. From miniature paintings to huge **sculptures**, art is a universal language to unite people and inspire hope. Over the course of history, art historians have tried to organize all the different styles and types of art into categories, which we call art movements. Not all art fits neatly into these categories, but they serve as a helpful framework to understand how and when artists developed their unique works.

Art movements emerge and change because of many reasons, often linked to social, political, or economic factors, such as new discoveries, new inventions, wars, or even reactions against art itself.

You do not need to know about art to enjoy it, but learning about the **fascinating stories of artists** and art movements might help you enjoy it even more.

This book was developed from activities I do at home with my kids to introduce them to the world of art via fun, hands-on projects. It covers the period of modern art, running **from Impressionism to Minimalism**, offering clues to understand the contemporary art era we currently live in.

The aim of this book is to expose kids to the **freedom of creativity and the power of imagination**, not for kids to remember all the artist names or movements. The projects in this book use easy-to-find, cost-efficient materials and are meant to provide adult-child bonding for ages 3 through 6, or self-led fun learning for ages 6+.

Tips for Supporting Children

Champion Process

The process of creating and exploring art is more important than the final product!

Champion Mistakes

The key to success is the ability to learn from mistakes. Sometimes, you will need to encourage trial and error with the activities!

Champion
Connections

Encourage kids to make connections—between the artworks, artists, and with things around us.

Champion
Freedom

If a child deviates from or is not interested in making an activity, give them the freedom to create something of their own. Let them experiment; let them make a mess!

IMPRESSIONISM

Impressionism is a style of painting that began in France in the 1860s and became most popular in the 1870s and 1880s. Leading figures of the movement include Claude Monet (page 13), Camille Pissarro, Pierre-Auguste Renoir, and Edgar Degas (page 19). Impressionist painters did not paint from their imagination, literature, or history like most other painters of the nineteenth century. Instead, they painted what they saw around them: towns and landscapes where they lived and scenes of everyday life, like people doing the washing and ironing, ballet dancers warming up, and customers being served in a restaurant.

Impressionists wanted to capture light and weather, not just the shape of the **LANDSCAPE**. They wanted to convey the life of what they saw and the fleeting quality of time. They painted snow falling over a town, mist clouding a river, a wheat field bathed in sunshine, and water lilies floating on a pond. To capture what they saw at a particular time, they had to paint in smaller pictures so that the artist could carry them outdoors and paint "en plein air" (outside) rather than in a studio. They painted quickly, using thick brushstrokes and dabs of paint. They let the colors mix into each other on the **CANVAS** and did not paint in detail, preferring to capture an "impression" of the place or person before them.

CLAUDE MONET

1840–1926, France

Founder of Impressionism, a prolific painter of landscapes who often painted "en plein air," expressing his perceptions about nature

French artist Claude Monet loved to draw as a child—he even made some extra money drawing pictures of people when he was young!

When Monet entered a school for the arts, his mother was supportive, but his father wanted him to take over the family grocery business. Lucky for us that Monet followed his artistic passion!

Monet moved to Paris to study art and painted outdoor scenes. In 1872, he painted a harbor with very loose brushstrokes. Titled *Impression, Sunrise* and shown in an **EXHIBITION** with paintings by his friends, the artists became known as the Impressionists, interested in capturing light, time, and feeling in their work.

Monet is most well-known for his paintings of water lilies. He painted more than 250 artworks on this **SUBJECT**, inspired by his water garden at Giverny in France. He painted the lilies in all seasons, all types of weather, and all times of day for more than thirty years. Some of his paintings were done during a sad time in Monet's life, after his wife passed away and he lost his son to World War I. He used art to express his feelings. Can you add your emotions to your art, too?

PAPER POND LILIES

easy   hard   clean   messy

What you need:

bowl

blue food coloring

green EVA foam sheet

pink cupcake liners

yellow pipe cleaners

LET'S GET MESSY!

Step 1

Fill your bowl with a little water and add a few drops of blue food coloring.

Step 2

Cut some lily pads from your green EVA foam sheet. Flatten three or four cupcake liners for each water lily.

Step 3

Thread a pipe cleaner through the cupcake liners and the lily pad, twisting down at the top to form the stigma.

TRACE THE LEAVES!

Leaves come in all shapes and sizes. Feel free to trace the shapes provided here or create your own!

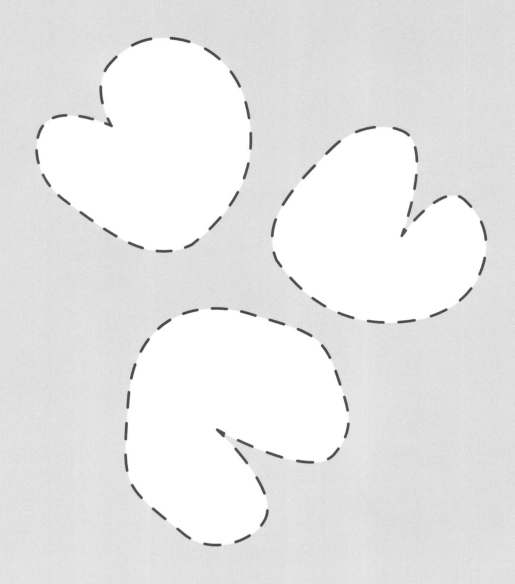

EDGAR DEGAS

1834–1917, France

A founder of the Impressionism movement, most famous for his pastel and oil paintings of ballet dancers and entertainers

Edgar Degas grew up in Paris, where his mother was an opera singer and his father was a banker.

Although he studied law, Degas showed great talent for drawing as a kid and decided to become an artist instead.

He wanted to experiment with new styles of painting and wasn't interested in painting what was popular at the time.

Together with other artists, Degas formed the Impressionists. But unlike the others, he spent time planning his paintings and making **SKETCHES** before starting to paint.

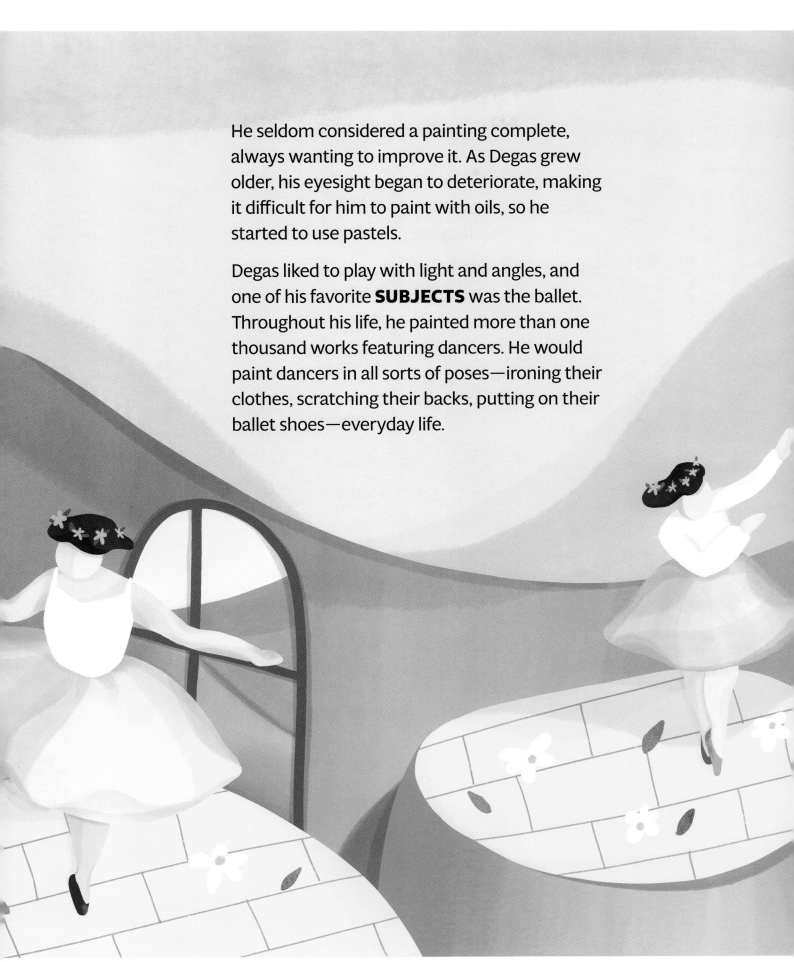

He seldom considered a painting complete, always wanting to improve it. As Degas grew older, his eyesight began to deteriorate, making it difficult for him to paint with oils, so he started to use pastels.

Degas liked to play with light and angles, and one of his favorite **SUBJECTS** was the ballet. Throughout his life, he painted more than one thousand works featuring dancers. He would paint dancers in all sorts of poses—ironing their clothes, scratching their backs, putting on their ballet shoes—everyday life.

STRIKE A POSE

easy   hard   clean   messy

What you need:

pencil

small mannequin

tissue paper

thin ribbon

paint and paintbrush

double-sided tape

scissors

MAKE A MASTERPIECE!

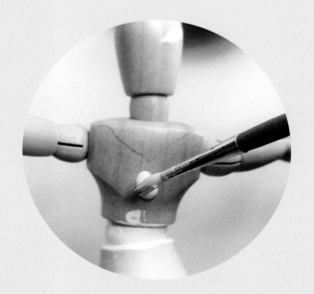

Step 1

On the mannequin, use a pencil to draw the bodice of the ballerina and then paint it in with your chosen paint color.

Step 2

Cut out a long rectangle of tissue paper and accordion-fold it. Use double-sided tape to adhere the paper around the mannequin's waist to form the ballerina's tutu.

Step 3

Tie a ribbon to the top of the tutu, around the ballerina's waist. Decorate the bodice, tutu, and headpiece with any materials you like!

POST-IMPRESSIONISM

Impressionism (page 12) dominated the art world in France in the 1870s and 1880s. In the 1890s, however, a group of artists wanted to change the popular painting style and formed **Post-Impressionism**, a movement that included a wide range of different artistic styles. Four major artists led the movement—Paul Cézanne (page 25), Paul Gaugin, Vincent van Gogh (page 31), and Georges Seurat (page 37). Each artist extended Impressionism in his own way. Cézanne added energy and painterly brushstrokes; Gaugin rejected painting from nature; Seurat used a more scientific approach (called Neo-Impressionism); and Van Gogh developed a unique swirly style.

All of these artists shared an interest in exploring the emotions and personal views of themselves. Before them, painting was seen as a window into the world. For the Post-Impressionist artists, art was a window into the mind and soul of the artist. They believed that art was an expression of imagination, not a copy of real life. They valued memories and wanted to communicate messages from the artist. Furthermore, unlike the Impressionists who tried to capture natural light, the Post-Impressionist artists often used an artificial color palette. Their vivid colors gave a sense of dynamism to their work, embodying the artists' wild imaginations.

PAUL CÉZANNE

1839–1906, France

Father of Post-Impressionism; a keen observer of nature, figures, and still lifes, bridging Impressionism of the late nineteenth century and other styles of the early twentieth century

Paul Cézanne loved to swim, write poetry, play music, and take long walks in the countryside as a child. His love of painting started early, when he was ten years old. Cézanne often went on long adventures, painting LANDSCAPES and the rugged mountains.

The neighbors living nearby laughed at him, believing his pictures to be poorly done. One day, a picture dealer from Paris saw Cézanne's paintings and recognized a talent.

Cézanne sold many works and soon became famous, but the artist remained humble and continued to do what he loved best.

Cézanne used the light and bright colors that the Impressionists enjoyed, but was more interested in exploring how objects are made up. He used different colors and small brushstrokes to build up many planes that formed one object. His apples are not just red but made of many layers and colors—orange, yellow, green, and more!

He painted many things in nature and hundreds of **STILL LIFES**—everyday objects at home arranged with different fruits.

He would spend hours arranging the fruit until he was happy with the way it looked!

FRUITY PEBBLES

easy   hard   clean   messy

What you need:

fruits and household objects

pebbles

paints and paintbrushes

GET CREATIVE!

Step 1

Select some fruits and explore them. Look at the different shapes, colors, patterns, and planes of each fruit. Pick which stones to paint the fruits on. Choose a shape that resembles each fruit.

Step 2

Paint patterns, such as seeds, stripes, and leaves, on the stones you chose. Be sure to observe the fruit while painting. For more difficult patterns, such as a pineapple, adults can create dots for the child to join up. Let the painted stones dry.

Step 3

Find different objects at home, such as a basket, plate, jug, tablecloth, vase, or flowers. Experiment with different compositions to form your own still life!

PLAY WITH PATTERN!

Did you know there are
many patterns found in nature?
Next time you go out to explore,
remember to look out for the
patterns around you!

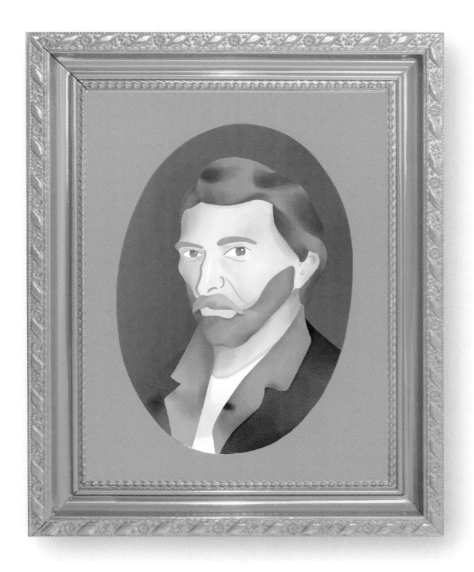

VINCENT VAN GOGH

1853–1890, the Netherlands

A Dutch Post-Impressionist painter and one of the most important figures in the history of Western art; known for his expressive, broken-up brushstrokes made in thick paint

Van Gogh learned to draw using pencils and charcoal sticks, and one of his favorite SUBJECTS to draw were poor, hardworking people.

Later, he started to use oil paints, but his paintings were dark and sad. It was his younger brother who introduced Impressionism (page 12) to Van Gogh, and he moved to Paris to learn from the artists creating Impressionist art.

There, he used brighter colors and his brushwork became more broken as he painted cafés and people on the streets. His paintings were full of curves and twirls, as if the paintings were moving.

He also became interested in painting **PORTRAITURES** of people. When he couldn't find models, he painted himself in the mirror for practice.

Later on, Van Gogh became sick, and even famously cut off his own ear, but he never stopped painting. In fact, he painted some of his most recognized works while in the hospital.

Although Van Gogh was not famous during his lifetime, today, he is considered one of the greatest and most influential artists!

SALTY NIGHT

easy   hard   clean   messy

What you need:

medium-size zip-top plastic bags

box or other small container

salt

cotton swabs

liquid food coloring

LET'S GET MESSY!

Step 1

Dye the salt different colors in zip-top plastic bags; I did eight. Put some salt into each bag and drip 10 to 15 drops of food coloring into each bag. Seal the bags and rub the color into the salt until it is evenly mixed. Little A was creative and used her feet, too!

Step 2

Lay out the salt in a box or other container to dry (I dried the salt overnight). I suggest placing the salt in the sunshine, or on a rainy day, seek help from a dehumidifier.

Step 3

Layer the different colors of salt. Make circles of yellow, orange, and red for the sun; green for trees; and dark blue for the evening sky. Use the cotton swabs to make swirls through the salt, and voilà!

SENSORY SAND

What you need:

2¾ cups (1 kg) fine sand

5 to 10 drops liquid food coloring

Paint stir stick

1½ cups (192 g) cornstarch

½ cup (120 ml) vegetable oil

1. Find a container, such as a baking dish or a shallow bucket, and pour in the sand. Add the food coloring until you have a color you like. Mix until fully incorporated into the sand.

2. Add the cornstarch and stir the sand and cornstarch until there is no more white color.

3. Pour in the oil and mix again until there are no dry parts. The oil should make the sand silky and moldable.

4. Scoop, mold, stamp, spoon, and get creative with your sensory sand!

GEORGES SEURAT

1859–1891, France

French Post-Impressionist artist most celebrated for painting in tiny dots, a style known as Pointillism, an exploration of color and the science of optics

Georges Seurat was a quiet child, and his parents always supported his passion for painting. With their help, he set up his own art studio near their house. For a while, Seurat painted with the Impressionists, but soon after, he began to explore the science of seeing and the beauty of color.

Instead of mixing colors on a palette, he would place small dots of color next to each other on the **CANVAS**. At a distance, the viewer's eye mixes the individual colors and the dots blend into different tones.

Seurat believed that dots, colors, and lines could create mood and emotion. Today, we call his way of painting **Pointillism,** pioneered by Seurat and his good friend Paul Signac.

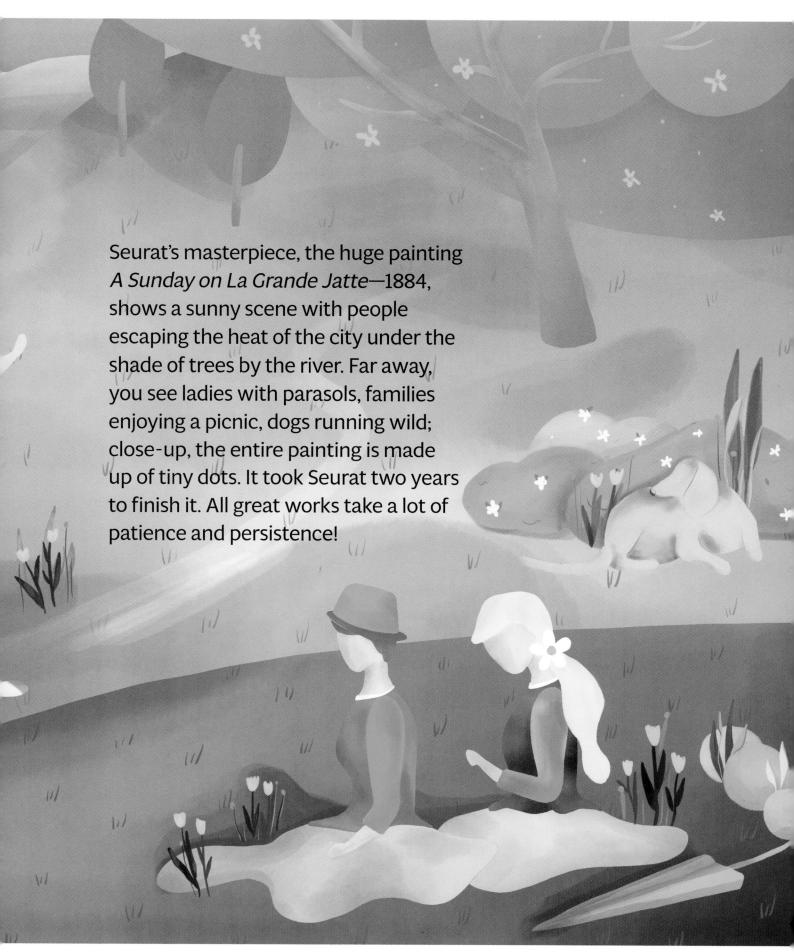

Seurat's masterpiece, the huge painting *A Sunday on La Grande Jatte—1884*, shows a sunny scene with people escaping the heat of the city under the shade of trees by the river. Far away, you see ladies with parasols, families enjoying a picnic, dogs running wild; close-up, the entire painting is made up of tiny dots. It took Seurat two years to finish it. All great works take a lot of patience and persistence!

BUTTON BAY

easy   hard   clean   messy

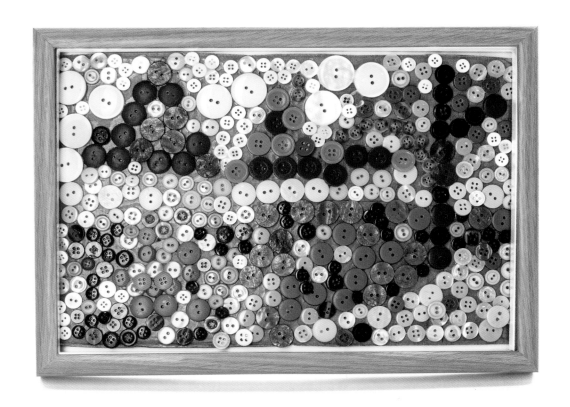

What you need:

cardboard

pencil

liquid glue

buttons in different sizes and colors

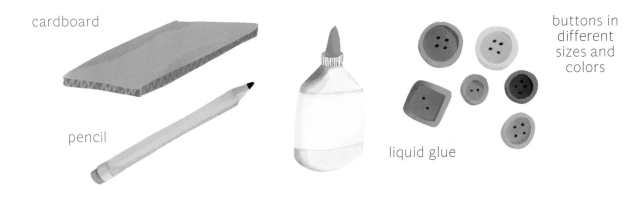

MAKE A MASTERPIECE!

Step 1

On the cardboard, sketch your landscape in pencil. Our example was created by a four-year-old and features a riverbank, river with a boat, mountains, and clouds.

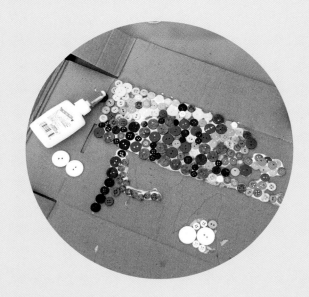

Step 2

Glue the buttons onto the cardboard. I recommend using different shades of each color for every section, much like Seurat did. Let dry.

Step 3

Once complete and dried, frame and hang your masterpiece!

VIENNA SECESSION

In 1897, a group of artists in Vienna, Austria, had had enough of popular conservative art. They were tired of looking at and painting realistic scenes used throughout art history. They wanted to make a change. They wanted to paint with **SYMBOLS** and bright colors. So, this group of artists, led by Gustav Klimt (page 43), set up their own movement called the **Vienna Secession**. "Secession" here means the breaking away of younger, more radical artists from an existing art group to form a new society.

The Vienna Secession was founded to promote innovation in contemporary art and its members encouraged artistic freedom more than creating art in any one style. As such, the movement included not only painters, but also sculptors, designers, and architects. Other key members included Josef Hoffmann, Koloman Moser, Egon Schiele, and Otto Wagner. Together, they marked the beginning of modern art in Austria. They even built a dedicated **EXHIBITION** setting, as well as published an official journal, to introduce their art to the world. The Vienna Secession's work is often linked to the larger Art Nouveau movement across Europe and has served as the beginnings of modern design.

GUSTAV KLIMT

1862–1918, Austria

An Austrian symbolist painter
most famous for his brightly colored
decorative paintings, often depicting
opulently gilded figures

Gustav Klimt was born to a poor immigrant family. His father and brother were gold engravers, and Klimt started off painting MURALS.

But when both his father and brother died when Klimt was just thirty, the loss changed his style of painting. He didn't want to paint history pictures anymore, but wanted to explore themes of the mind and paint pictures of women.

He joined the Vienna Secession group and was one of its most important leaders. But ten years later, after a trip to Italy where Klimt saw Byzantine art, he started his famous Gold Period—paintings made with lots of gold color and gold leaf.

Klimt worked slowly and carefully on each painting—he painted all day, every day. The clothing his female subjects wore was often **ABSTRACT,** formed in shapes in reds, blues, greens, and gold, filled with organic forms like spirals and flowers. Some of Klimt's most famous works, such as *The Kiss*, are now highly sought after!

What events or places that you have visited have made an impression on you?

KISS FROM THE HEART

 easy   hard   clean   messy

What you need:

small plastic bowl

liquid glue (optional)

transparent acrylic sheet

MOD PODGE

Mod Podge

eco-friendly gold glitter

mosaic tiles

sponge tool

11 × 17-inch (A3, or 27.5 × 42.5 m) color printout of *The Kiss*

GET CREATIVE!

Step 1

Make your own glitter glue by mixing the Mod Podge with ample gold glitter in a small plastic bowl. On a flat work surface, place the acrylic sheet on top of the Klimt printout. Use the sponge tool to paint the gold glitter onto the acrylic sheet, leaving only the figures uncovered.

Step 2

Decorate the figures' hair and clothing with a range of mosaic tiles, using glue or Mod Podge to adhere them to the acrylic sheet.

Step 3

Print out a portrait of yourself in about the same size, and insert it between your acrylic sheet and the Klimt printout. Secure and frame!

FAUVISM

Fauvism, which means "the wild beasts" in French, was the name of a modern **ART MOVEMENT** that began in France in 1905, led by the painters Henri Matisse (page 49) and André Derain. Many people didn't like this new movement, because the artists' approach to painting was so unrefined compared to art that was popular at the time. An art critic coined the name and it was not meant as a compliment. The group was together for only three years, from 1905 to 1907, after which many artists moved on to other styles.

The Fauvists were influenced by the bright colors used by Post-Impressionist artists Vincent van Gogh (page 31) and Paul Gaugin. They used bright, expressive colors and painted in fierce, exaggerated brushstrokes. In fact, color was the most important aspect of a Fauvist painting, but their colors were chosen based on feeling and their memory of an experience. Fauvists also shifted away from urban themes and returned to Impressionist **SUBJECTS**—leisure scenes and country **LANDSCAPES**—simplifying their drawings with only a few details. Instead, their paintings create an illusion of depth and a sense of volume through an overall decorative pattern of colors.

HENRI MATISSE

1869–1954, France

One of the world's most admired painters,
known for his ability to unite color and line
in his art; also recognized for his late cutouts,
described as "drawing with scissors"

Henri Matisse grew up in the northern part of France. Like Paul Cézanne (page 25), Matisse went to school in Paris and studied law. He passed the bar exam in 1888 and took a clerk job at a law firm. The next year, however, Matisse became ill with appendicitis. His mother bought him some art supplies to keep him occupied during his recovery.

Matisse fell in love with painting and decided to pursue the path of an artist. He experimented with different painting styles and did not want to follow how other artists painted. He learned from masters such as Vincent van Gogh (page 31), Paul Cézanne (page 25), and Georges Seurat (page 37), and by the early 1900s, Matisse developed a new painting style called **Fauvism**, marked by bright colors and energetic brushwork.

As Matisse grew older, his eyesight started to deteriorate. Never one to give up, Matisse began to use brightly painted paper and scissors to cut out shapes—animals, birds, dancers, flowers, leaves—and arranged them in large **COLLAGES** to bring his art to life. He called this "drawing with scissors." Matisse's works continue to be highly sought after today!

Would you give up easily if things didn't go your way? Or would you work hard, like Matisse?

PRINT GARDEN

easy   hard   clean   messy

What you need:

plain white paper

pencil

8½ × 11-inch (A4, or 21.25 × 27.5 cm) plastic folders

paints and paintbrush

foam paper

scissors

liquid glue

LET'S GET MESSY!

Step 1

Draw your own leaf templates on plain paper, then cut them out. Use the templates to cut out different leaf shapes from the foam paper. Adhere the foam leaves to the plastic folder sheets with glue.

Step 2

Cut out the plastic leaf shapes with generous borders to make your "stamps."

Step 3

Paint your foam leaf shapes and print/ press the painted side onto a piece of plain paper and arrange the composition as you wish!

ORPHISM

Orphism was an **ART MOVEMENT** in Paris that emerged around 1912. Pioneered by the couple Robert and Sonia Delaunay (page 55), Orphism was influenced by both an art style called Cubism and color theory. The name "Orphism" comes from a famous ancient Greek poet and musician, Orpheus, and points to the idea that painting can be like music, with the ability to evoke emotions while reaching abstraction.

Unlike the muted colors of Cubism, Orphists arranged bright, complementary colors in their work to create rhythm, movement, and energy. Orphism was also more **ABSTRACT** than previous art styles and rarely featured figures, focusing more on shape and color. Robert Delaunay used the term "simultanism" to describe his work and believed that colors could look different depending on the colors around them. The Delaunays' paintings used overlapping circles, in contrasting yet subtle colors, that bring out the vibrancy of their **CANVASES**.

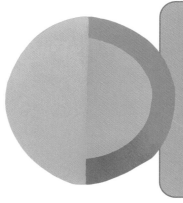

Orphists also experimented with different art forms. From poetry to design, some of the movement's most famous works were Sonia Delaunay's textile designs in fashion and interior decor. Although a short-lived movement, Orphism helped encourage collaborations between artists and other industries, such as fashion, design, and decor.

SONIA DELAUNAY

1885–1979, Ukraine

Ukrainian-born French painter famous for her
bold and colorful geometric art and textiles

Sonia Delaunay was born in Ukraine. At five years old, she was sent to live with her uncle and aunt in Russia. There, she had a good education, visited museums, and traveled a lot. When she was sixteen, her art teacher thought she was talented and encouraged her to go to Germany to study painting. From there, she went to Paris, excited about the art world. Her childhood memories of Ukraine, however, would stay with her, especially the bright colors and costumes of Ukrainian weddings.

She met her husband, Robert Delaunay, and together they pioneered the simultanism style within Orphism. Inspired by Cubism, but focused more on color, Sonia Delaunay experimented with matching primary and secondary colors to create contrasts.

She believed that the same color could look different depending on the colors next to it. Concentric circles are her trademark, bringing movement, rhythm, and even musical qualities to her pictures.

Sonia Delaunay is not just famous for her expressive **ABSTRACT** paintings, many inspired by the busy streets of Paris, but also for expanding her creativity into designing, making, and selling clothes, swimsuits, and textiles.

She was so successful she was the first living female artist to have a big **EXHIBITION** at the Louvre Museum in Paris!

DELICIOUS LOLLIPOPS

easy   hard   clean   messy

What you need:

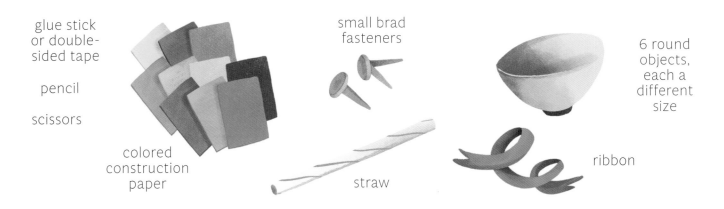

glue stick
or double-
sided tape

pencil

scissors

colored
construction
paper

small brad
fasteners

straw

6 round
objects,
each a
different
size

ribbon

MAKE A MASTERPIECE!

Step 1

Find six different round objects at home, each a different size. Trace each object onto two different colors of construction paper.

Step 2

Cut out all your round shapes. For each size, cut one circle in half and leave one whole. With a glue stick or tape, stick the half circle onto the whole one. Repeat for all the sizes.

Step 3

Layer and stick your circles together. Or for twistable layers, pierce the middle with a pencil and combine with a fastener. Tape a straw to the back of your lollipop and tie on a piece of ribbon for decoration!

FUTURISM

Futurism was an **ART MOVEMENT** that started in Italy in 1909. Using different types of **MEDIUM**, from painting to **SCULPTURE**, from music to textiles, Futurist artists captured the energy and dynamism of the modern world. Their themes explored the future, and they admired speed, technology, youth, cars, airplanes, science, and the city. Futurism focused on the movement of an object, overlaying the patterns many times to understand the motion it creates. Color, line, and shape are all important elements in Futurist artists' works.

Futurism was launched by an Italian writer, Filippo Tommaso Marinetti. Other key artists included Giacomo Balla (page 61), Umberto Boccioni, and Gino Severini. The Futurists wanted to separate themselves from the past, and they promoted themselves as young and strong. They were influenced by Cubism, but their works appeared even more abstract. After World War I, however, many artists rejected this approach, preferring to return to a more traditional way of painting.

GIACOMO BALLA

1871–1958, Italy

Key proponent of Futurism, known for his geometric paintings that championed light, movement, and speed

Giacomo Balla was the son of an industrial chemist and studied music as a child. By age twenty, he decided to follow his interest in art and studied painting. He worked as an illustrator and caricaturist in Rome, Italy, and even showed his art at major EXHIBITIONS in Europe.

Balla was influenced by Filippo Tommaso Marinetti's Futurist **MANIFESTO** and began to use the Futurism style, focusing on light, movement, and speed. Later, he began to design and paint Futurist furniture, clothing, and **SCULPTURES.**

In late 1912, Balla began to explore the motion and speed of racing automobiles and created an important series that suggests the passage of a car through a **LANDSCAPE**.

Using crisscrossing lines, planes, and color, his paintings were **ABSTRACT**, but with a noticeable story.

JET SET TO SPACE!

easy   hard   clean   messy

What you need:

single-hole punch

scissors

long pole

small plastic disposable bowl

paints and paintbrushes

thin cardstock

thin string or thread

large piece of cardstock

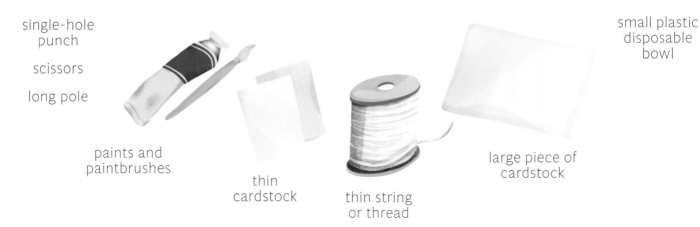

GET CREATIVE!

Step 1

Twist the thin cardstock into a small cone and punch two holes at the open end. Ensure the bottom opening tip is very small by twisting the cone tightly. Tape the cone together.

Step 2

Using string or thread woven through the holes you punched, tie the cone to a long pole. Secure the pole with tape, or have someone hold it upright on a table, and dangle the stringed cone over the edge of a tabletop, close to your large piece of paper on the floor.

Step 3

In a small bowl, dilute some paint with a little water (you may need to test the consistency), and pour the paint into the cone. Push the cone gently to attain a swinging pendulum effect. Repeat with more colors! Add a rocket to complete your space travel, if you like!

ADD-ON ROCKET

easy   hard   clean   messy

What you need:

paints and paintbrush

scissors

cardboard

black paper

recycled plastic water bottle

shredded red and yellow crepe paper

double-sided tape

aluminum foil

LET'S GET MESSY!

Step 1

Create a rocket by painting a recycled water bottle. Wrap the cap in aluminum foil (or make a short cone for the rocket head). Cut out two fin shapes from the cardboard and paint them as you like.

Step 2

For your rocket window, cut out two small circles from the black paper, one slightly larger than the other. Wrap the larger circle in aluminum foil. Tape the circles together. For thrusters, make two short cylinders from black paper and tape them together.

Step 3

Assemble all the pieces onto the body of your rocket using double-sided tape. Tape the shredded crepe paper to your thrusters and your fiery rocket is fit to zoom through your cosmic universe!

DADAISM

During World War I, many artists, writers and thinkers came together in Switzerland. Influenced by **ART MOVEMENTS** before them, such as Futurism (page 60), these artists made cutting-edge works in poetry, music, art, theater, and dance. Together, they formed **Dada**, a movement that protested against the horrors of war and questioned the society that started it.

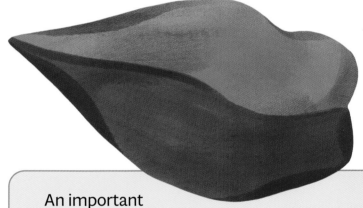

For Dada artists, the focus was to make works that challenged norms and asked difficult questions, rather than to create something beautiful. Key artists of the movement included Hugo Ball, Marcel Duchamp, Hans Arp, Sophie Taeuber-Arp (page 69), Hannah Höch (page 74), and Man Ray. They experimented with new materials and collaging, adding chance and randomness into their works. Their art was infused with humor and satire, yet asked serious questions about the role of art in the modern world.

An important innovation of Dadaism was the ready-made, everyday objects taken out of context and presented as "art," with little creativity from the artist. Duchamp, for example, used a urinal as a **SCULPTURE**, simply signing his name on it! This questioned what art really was and the role of the artist in creating it. The ideals of Dadaism soon spread to Berlin, Germany, New York, and Paris and formed the basis of Surrealism (page 86).

SOPHIE TAEUBER-ARP

1889–1943, Switzerland

One of the most important artists to bridge
the gap between fine art and craft

Sophie Taeuber-Arp was a Swiss artist and key figure of the Dada movement. She studied textile design in Germany and was inspired by Cubism. She experimented with many art forms, including painting, SCULPTURE, tapestry, dance, writing, fashion, and interior design.

Breaking down barriers between fine art and craft, she believed that decoration can also be the art of everyday life.

Against the backdrop of World War I, Dadaism objected to the refined style of art and preferred a simpler way of creating. Although a leading member of this group, Taeuber-Arp created colorful abstractions,

instead of the angry **COLLAGES** her peers were making. She played with shapes and colors, adding curves and arcs, and moving them around freely to let **COMPOSITIONS** emerge by chance. Her **ABSTRACT** paintings were full of energy, like music on **CANVAS**, and reminded people that, in tough times, joy and freedom do exist.

Taeuber-Arp pushed the limits of abstraction in art and helped transform craft into an art form. She remains a strong female voice who dared to challenge what was accepted.

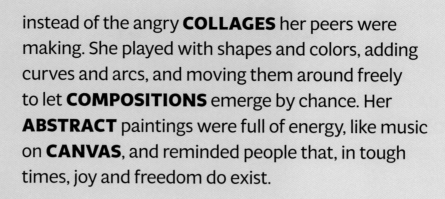

Would you speak out and fight for what you believe?

ARP FLAPS

easy ▬▬▬ hard   clean ▬ messy

What you need:

colored paper

double-sided tape

scissors

Make a Masterpiece!

Step 1

Fold one piece of colored paper in half like a book. On the right inner page, form quadrants by cutting up different colored paper and taping the pieces down. Cut a pattern on the left page to form a shape on top of one of your quadrants.

Step 2

Fold three more pieces of colored paper in half. You should have one piece folded on the left side, and two on the right side. Draw and cut out shapes so each quadrant has a different pattern on top.

Step 3

Assemble your sheets like a book and adhere them together along the spine using double-sided tape. Your Arp-inspired collage flaps are ready!

MATCH THE COLORS!

Did you know
opposite colors on the
color wheel are called
"complementary" colors?

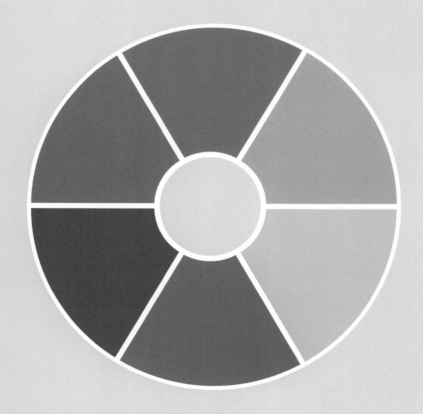

Red <-> **Green**

Blue <-> **Orange**

Yellow <-> **Purple**

Hannah Höch

1889–1978, Germany

A pioneer of photomontage and a key member of the Berlin, Germany, Dada movement

As a young German artist, Hannah Höch studied glass design, graphic design, and block printing, but soon started to experiment with COLLAGE and photomontage while working at a magazine publishing house in Berlin, Germany. In this technique, she would cut up images from popular magazines and recombine them in a dynamic and layered style.

The busy, overlapping pictures reflect the chaos of the postwar era.

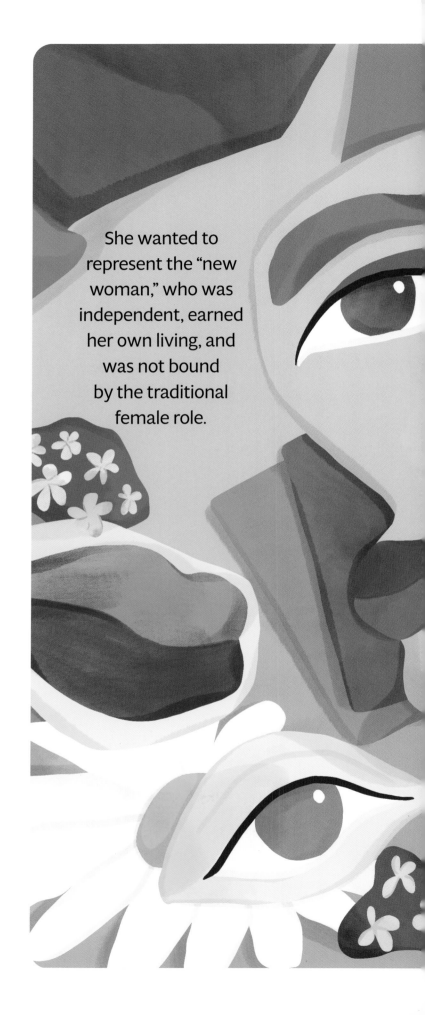

She wanted to represent the "new woman," who was independent, earned her own living, and was not bound by the traditional female role.

As an important member of Dadaism, she overturned the art conventions of painting and **SCULPTURE** as well as the social roles of women. Her art captures the rebellious spirit of the new age.

Although Höch received acclaim for her work, her male peers considered her only an amateur artist. Today, Höch is known as a feminist icon who strived to make women equal to men. Her legacy was to use art as a means to challenge and change the norms of society.

MESSAGE MONTAGE

easy   hard   clean   messy

What you need:

cardstock

washi
tape

scissors

old
magazines

glue

GET CREATIVE!

Step 1

Think of a story you want to tell or a theme you wish to explore. Choose images from magazines that help tell your story and cut them out. Inspired by Hannah Höch, we chose images that represent the strength of women.

Step 2

Play around with your composition, overlapping different photo fragments, until you are happy with it.

Step 3

Use tape to stick down your pieces onto cardstock and add blocks and strips of color with washi tape and paper. Your photomontage is ready—go and spread your message!

DE STIJL

De Stijl (pronounced *duh-stayl*) was an **ART MOVEMENT** in the Netherlands that lasted from 1917 to around 1931 pioneered by two of the group's most famous artists, Piet Mondrian (page 81) and Theo van Doesburg. "De Stijl" means "style" in Dutch, and these artists wanted to simplify their paintings as much as possible, leaving only lines and simple colors. Their works were treated like grids, with squares and rectangles formed by a careful arrangement of horizontal and vertical lines. Some of these grids were then filled with primary colors—red, yellow, and blue—next to black, white, and gray.

De Stijl artists published a **MANIFESTO** in which Mondrian expressed his ideas on art, and named their type of **ABSTRACT** art Neo-Plasticism. The journal helped spread their theories to architecture, involving key architects J. J. P. Oud and Gerrit Rietveld. Although the De Stijl movement was confined to the Netherlands, because the country was not involved in World War I and the group of artists could not leave the country during the war, their work still had a big influence on the development of abstract art and modern architecture, such as the Bauhaus movement and the international style.

PIET MONDRIAN

1872–1944, the Netherlands

Dutch painter and a founder of the De Stijl
movement, best known for his unique style
of simplifying compositions into grids of black
lines filled with primary colors

Piet Mondrian was a Dutch modern artist of the De Stijl group. Mondrian was exposed to art at a very young age by his father and uncle, who were both artists.

At the start of his career, Mondrian was teaching and painting at the same time, mostly realistic **LANDSCAPES**, especially trees and fields in the Netherlands.

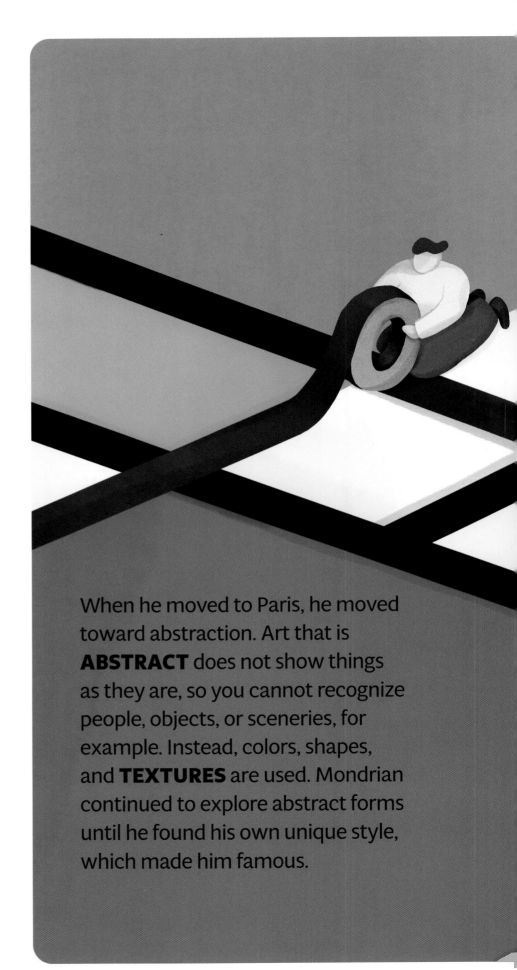

When he moved to Paris, he moved toward abstraction. Art that is **ABSTRACT** does not show things as they are, so you cannot recognize people, objects, or sceneries, for example. Instead, colors, shapes, and **TEXTURES** are used. Mondrian continued to explore abstract forms until he found his own unique style, which made him famous.

Mondrian always mixed his own colors, never using paint directly from a tube. He often used white and primary colors—red, yellow, and blue—and placed them in a grid of black lines that he created without a ruler!

Mondrian painted about 250 of these **GEOMETRIC** abstracts and called his style Neo-Plasticism. His paintings became so famous that many people, advertisers, architects, and fashion and furniture designers around the world were influenced by his style.

MONDRIAN PUZZLE

easy   hard   clean   messy

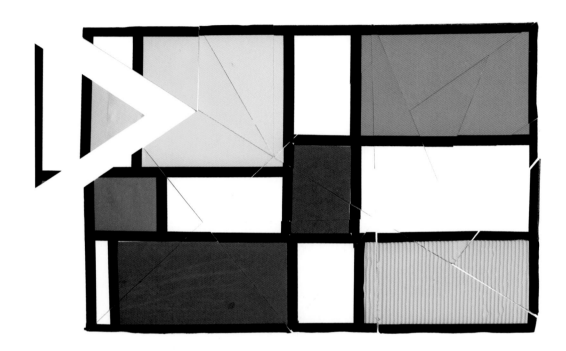

What you need:

pencil

red, yellow, and blue colored paper

black washi tape

white cardstock

liquid glue

square and rectangular objects

scissors

LET'S GET MESSY!

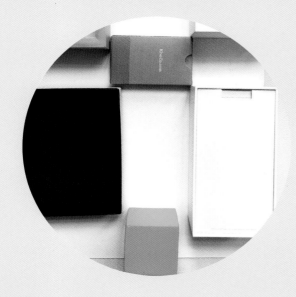

Step 1

Find rectangular and square objects of different sizes around the house. Place them onto your white cardstock until you are happy with the composition, leaving some parts of the paper uncovered. Now, trace the shapes.

Step 2

Trace the same shapes onto your colored paper. Cut out the shapes and glue them onto the white card. Glue down the whole shape, not just the edges. Then, encase the colored shapes with black washi tape to form your grid.

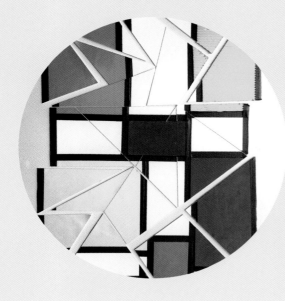

Step 3

Turn the white cardstock to the blank side. Decide how many puzzle pieces you would like and draw out dividing shapes. Ask an adult to help cut out your puzzle!

SURREALISM

Surrealism is an **ART MOVEMENT** that flourished in the 1920s and 1930s in Europe, born out of an earlier movement called Dadaism (page 68). This was after the horrors of World War I, perhaps a protest at the destruction caused by civilized life. Instead, the artists found magic in the unexpected. Surrealist artists painted amazing and unusual things. They painted their dreams, random thoughts, and anything that came to mind. They wanted to celebrate imagination because they felt the world around them was too strict and that it needed more curiosity.

So, artists like Salvador Dalí, Max Ernst, Joan Miró, René Magritte (page 87), and Frida Kahlo (page 93) explored these ideas in their art. There are two main types of Surrealist art. First, art that is inspired by dreams—where the artist painted bizarre scenes that would never happen in real life. People floating in air, gigantic apples stuck in a room, magically disappearing people and animals, clocks turning backward. These fantasies are surprising, and unrelated items are placed next to each other for no clear reason. The second type of Surrealism is called automatism—art made without thinking—such as Miró's playful works that seem like colorful doodles. All the artists' works are full of surprises and Surrealism influenced much later art, especially Abstract Expressionism (page 98).

RENÉ MAGRITTE

1898–1967, Belgium

Prominent Surrealist painter known for giving new meanings to everyday objects, such as clouds and green apples, by placing them in unusual contexts

René Magritte was a Surrealist painter who wanted people to look at everyday things in different ways.

Magritte studied at art school and took many jobs designing advertisements, posters, and wallpaper to earn money. During World War II, Magritte experimented with Fauvism (page 48) and Futurism (page 60), making a living while trying to find his own style.

Critics did not like Magritte's art. But as the Surrealists became more popular, so did he.

Today, Magritte is well-known for painting ordinary objects, such as apples, birds, candles, clocks, and eggs, as well as windows, mirrors, men in suits, doors, clouds, and bowler hats!

Although these don't sound strange, it is the placement of these objects that makes his paintings bizarre. You might see an oversized apple taking up an entire room; or a face made of sky; or men with umbrellas walking through hanging doors. These bold **COMPOSITIONS** grab your attention and surprise you. They speak to the power of imagination and often appear dreamlike.

Have you ever had a dream where everything is upside down or inside out?

DREAM BOX

easy   hard   clean   messy

What you need:

paint and
paintbrush

cotton
balls

white
cardstock

green apple

bowler hat, or
other hat, and suit,
preferably black

box

scissors

double-
sided tape

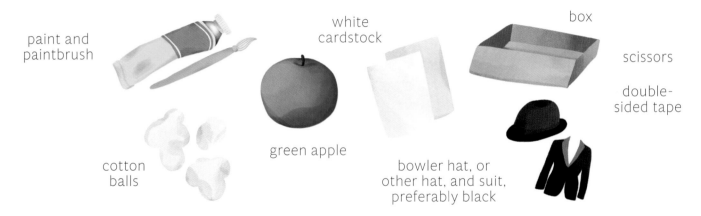

MAKE A MASTERPIECE!

Step 1

Cut a large open window from your box. Ask an adult to help, if needed. Paint the inside of the box a sky blue color. Let dry. Once dry, use double-sided tape to stick on cotton balls as the clouds.

Step 2

Dress up in a suit and hat. Bite into an apple and hold it there. Ask an adult to take a photo of you.

Step 3

Ask an adult to print out the picture to about three-quarters of your box's size. Tape cardstock to the back of the photo for support and cut around the edges of the image. Stick it in front of the clouds!

COIN TOSS & DRAW!

Get ready to let your imagination run wild!
Grab a coin, toss it onto the grid, and in 30
seconds, draw a surrealist scene with the icon
you landed on! The more ridiculous and absurd
your depiction, the more fun the game will be!

FRIDA KAHLO

1907–1954, Mexico

Strong woman who overcame many
difficulties to become one of the world's
most famous artists

Frida Kahlo was born in Mexico and grew up in a house called "la Casa Azul," the Blue House, with her parents and six sisters. The house is now the Frida Kahlo Museum. Kahlo loved to draw when she was young, often preferring to be alone than to play with her sisters.

At age six, she caught a disease called polio, which hurt her right leg. At age eighteen, she was badly injured in a bus accident and lay in bed recovering for many months.

During her life, Kahlo had many health problems that caused her a lot of pain, but she always continued to paint. She used her art, many examples of which are **SELF-PORTRAITS**, to show people about her suffering and her feelings, especially not being able to have children.

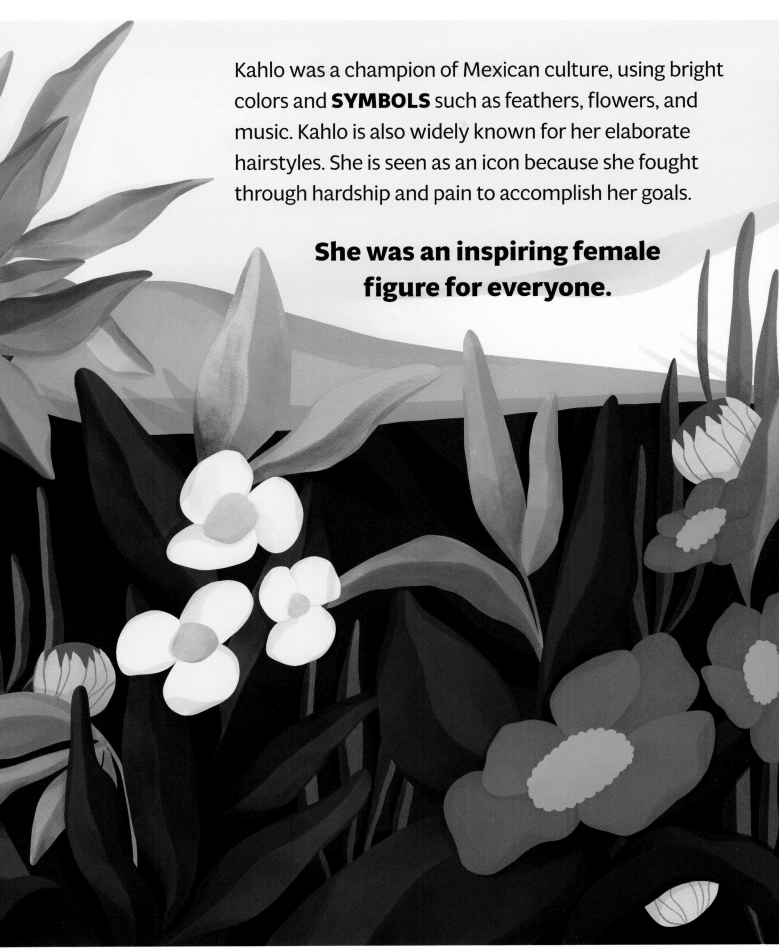

Kahlo was a champion of Mexican culture, using bright colors and **SYMBOLS** such as feathers, flowers, and music. Kahlo is also widely known for her elaborate hairstyles. She is seen as an icon because she fought through hardship and pain to accomplish her goals.

She was an inspiring female figure for everyone.

FRIDA CROWN

easy ▬▬▭ hard   clean ▬▬▭ messy

What you need:

stapler and
staples

scissors

paints and
paintbrush

egg carton

hot glue gun
and glue

white
cardstock

GET CREATIVE!

Step 1

Cut up your empty egg carton. Keep both the egg cups and the divider pieces in the middle. Cut leaf shapes from the carton's flap. Ask an adult to help you with the cutting, if needed.

Step 2

Paint your cut-up pieces in bright, bold colors and let dry. Once dried, use a glue gun to attach the smaller pieces inside the egg cups to form the flower stamen.

Step 3

Cut a piece of cardstock long enough to form a circle around your head. Carefully staple it to fit. Then, use a glue gun to stick your flowers and leaves onto the front of your crown!

ABSTRACT EXPRESSIONISM

The **Abstract Expressionism** movement began in the 1940s in New York City after World War II. Although **ABSTRACT** art has no **SUBJECT**, just lines, shapes, and colors, the Abstract Expressionists tried to convey feelings and emotions through their paintings. There were two main groups within the movement: action painters, such as Jackson Pollock, who used large brushes to make busy paint marks, famously putting his big **CANVASES** on the floor to throw and pour paint on; and color field painters, such as Mark Rothko (page 99) and Helen Frankenthaler, who filled their canvases with big areas of single colors, creating simple **COMPOSITIONS** that invite meditation. Although they had such different styles, these artists all used very large canvases and an "all over" approach, which means the whole painting is treated with equal importance.

Abstract Expressionism was the first American movement to gain worldwide influence and put New York City at the center of the art world. Before then, Paris had always led the way. The movement showed how much energy and creativity the United States had, and that it did not need to follow in Europe's footsteps. By the 1960s, however, Abstract Expressionism had lost its influence and new movements came in, such as Pop Art (page 104) and Minimalism (page 116).

MARK ROTHKO

1903–1970, Latvia

American painter of Latvian Jewish descent,
who considered his fields of color to be a
form of communication, to move people
and express human emotions

Mark Rothko was born in Latvia but moved to America when he was ten years old, where he later went on to study at Yale University. He dropped out, though, in his second year and moved to New York where he set his mind to becoming an artist.

There, he learned about the work of Henri Matisse (page 49) and even tried his hand at Surrealism (page 86).

With World War II underway, he became part of a group of young artists who thought that following artistic traditions was irrelevant. They wanted to promote **ABSTRACT** art, and Rothko's paintings are often considered to be Abstract Expressionist, although he disagreed with that label.

At the time, Rothko's paintings were completely new. He is most well-known for his "color field" paintings—large **CANVASES** painted with blurry-edged rectangles, as though they are floating on a field of color.

The goal of these oversized canvases was to engulf the viewer within the painting, to invite visual and emotional contemplation. Rothko always felt that art is spiritual, can paint human emotions, and provides space for reflection.

MINI ROTHKO

 easy   hard   clean   messy

What you need:

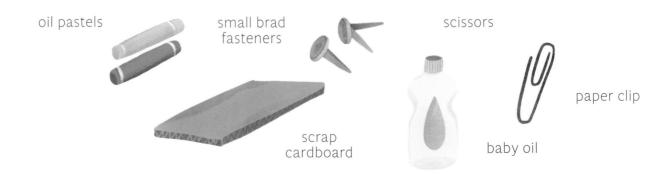

oil pastels   small brad fasteners   scissors   paper clip

scrap cardboard   baby oil

LET'S GET MESSY!

Step 1

Cut out a circle from cardboard and divide the circle into six segments. To make your color wheel, color your segments in red, orange, yellow, green, blue, and purple. Carefully poke a hole in the middle and attach a paper clip with a fastener.

Step 2

Cut out at least four rectangular cardboard pieces. Spin your color wheel and draw a small rectangle shape onto your cardboard in the color you land on. Repeat so you have two or three colored rectangles and a color to fill the edges for each rectangle.

Step 3

Dip your finger in some baby oil and rub each segment of color on the rectangular pieces so it's fully blended. Try to use a different finger for each color so they don't turn dark and muddy. Hang your mini Rothkos to be admired!

POP ART

Pop Art was a fun **ART MOVEMENT** that exploded in the 1950s and 1960s. Young artists wanted to make art that was available to everyone, using images that anyone could recognize and relate to. It was also a reaction to the seriousness of Abstract Expressionism (page 98) that came before them. Pop artists turned to movies, advertising, product packaging, pop music, and comic books for their art. This was the period after World War II, when people spent a lot of money, making mass-produced items popular. Moreover, the television replaced the radio as the main information outlet. So, movie stars and store-bought products became the objects of attention.

Pop artists used bright, vibrant colors, generally presented with humor or irony. Andy Warhol (page 105), the most famous Pop artist, created **SCREEN PRINTS** that repeated the same image over and over, such as banknotes, soup cans, ketchup bottles, and celebrities like Marilyn Monroe, all popular American "products." Roy Lichtenstein used Ben-Day dots (a printing method that uses dots to create shading and add color) to create his special comic strip–style paintings, whereas English artists David Hockney and Peter Blake also made Pop works. As the art world shifted toward installations in the 1970s, however, Pop Art became less popular, but to this day, its influence continues to find its way into fashion, music, and more.

ANDY WARHOL

1928–1987, United States of America

Leading Pop Art figure,
famous for creating screen prints of
celebrities and mass-produced products,
repeating the images over and over,
making art available to everyone

Andy Warhol is one of the world's most famous artists.

When he was eight years old, he developed a liver disease that caused his limbs to spasm. During his recovery, his mother taught him to draw. After graduating university, Warhol moved to New York City to work as a commercial artist, where he came up with many award-winning advertisements.

Warhol soon became interested in exploring popular culture in his work, reproducing images of mass-produced goods like Coca-Cola bottles and Campbell's soup cans over and over. He called it Pop Art. Warhol also used pictures of famous people and would repeat the same **PORTRAITURE** again and again, using different and contrasting colors every time.

He used a method called screen printing, which uses a blocking stencil marked on fine fabric mesh and stretched over a wooden frame. Ink is then applied and passes through the stencil to create a **PRINT**.

Warhol was a unique artist. He wanted to be rich and famous, and he became a celebrity. He exhibited a very personal style, with shocking white hair, wearing black with glasses or sunglasses. Today, he remains a legend, revolutionizing art as products everyone could afford.

What inspires you in your everyday life?

RECYCLED TRAY PRINT

 easy   hard   clean   messy

 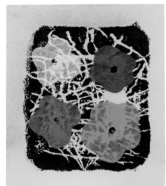 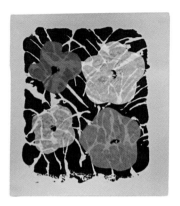

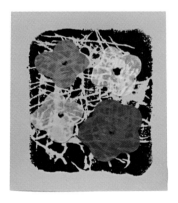 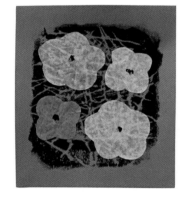 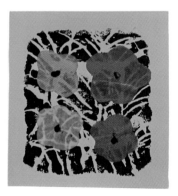

What you need:

foam meat
or vegetable
tray, washed
and dried

double-
sided tape

brayer

block print
inks or paint

tissue
paper

colored
paper

pencil

scissors

plastic tray
or A4 folder

MAKE A MASTERPIECE!

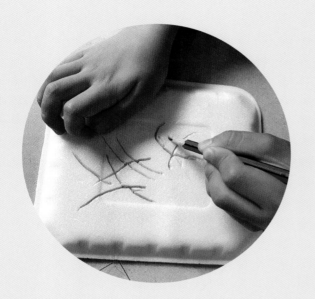

Step 1

On the bottom side of your clean foam tray, etch in lines and curves with a pencil to resemble grass. Roll your brayer in block print ink (or paint) on a plastic tray or A4 folder so the brayer is covered evenly with a thin coat.

Step 2

Roll the ink onto your etched tray. Press a piece of colored paper onto the ink to transfer the image to the paper. Repeat this process so you have the same picture on a few other colors of paper. Let dry.

Step 3

Cut out flower shapes from your colored tissue paper and use tape to stick them onto your prints. For the flower stamen, dab your pinky in a tiny bit of ink or paint and gently dot the color onto the center of your flowers!

EXPRESS YOUR EMOTIONS

Everyone has emotions, but they are not always obvious to others. Learn how to describe your emotions to help others understand how you feel!

HAPPY **SAD** **ANGRY**

ANNOYED **SHOCKED** **SHY**

CORITA KENT

1918–1986, United States of America

The Pop Art nun, a teacher and artist
advocating hope through colorful
compositions and slogans

Corita Kent, also known as Sister Mary Corita, was an innovative artist and teacher. She entered the religious order Immaculate Heart of Mary at age eighteen. As a nun, she went to see Andy Warhol's EXHIBITION of soup can paintings and was inspired by his art. She was famously referred to as the Pop Art nun.

Kent produced brightly colored serigraphs, which she described as "drawing on silk," another term for silkscreen printing. Her colorful works used advertising slogans and popular song lyrics, but also quotes from the Bible, to spread messages about racism, poverty, and social injustice.

She was making art when consumer culture was exploding, so she would pick words like "burger" and "humble," cleverly including messages about the way we live and our duty to help other people.

Kent's experimental approach was not welcomed by the Church, which criticized her work, forcing her to leave her religion. But she didn't leave her art, continuing to reflect her experiences, and her battle with cancer through quieter images. Many of her messages are still important today.

Can you think of words that inspire hope?

SUNNY SLOGAN

easy   hard   clean   messy

What you need:

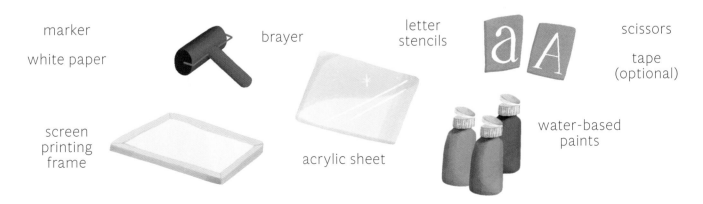

marker

white paper

brayer

screen printing frame

acrylic sheet

letter stencils

scissors

tape (optional)

water-based paints

GET CREATIVE!

Step 1

Using your marker draw a sun, or any shape you like, on the acrylic sheet. Cut out your shape. This will be the colored part of your print. Secure the acrylic sheet to the flat side of your screen print frame, taping it in place, if needed.

Step 2

Lay your frame, flat side, on top of your paper. Apply a generous amount of paint and spread it across the screen using your brayer, ensuring the cut-out part is covered in color. Let dry.

Step 3

Think of positive words like "hope," "love," or "light." Adhere letter stencils onto your sun image and paint them with bright colors to complete your slogan!

MINIMALISM

Minimalism is another **ART MOVEMENT** that emerged in New York in the 1960s. It, too, reacted against Abstract Expressionism (page 98) that came before, with the artists avoiding emotions and feelings in their art. Instead, the artists focused on the materiality of their works. The artists wanted viewers to not only see but also experience the works in front of them. They believed that **ABSTRACT** art has its own presence and does not need to represent anything else. Minimalist art has a sense of order and simplicity to it. The artists used factory-manufactured industrial materials and often repeated **GEOMETRIC** installations to make large artworks. By walking around the installation, viewers experience qualities like weight, height, and even light. This approach challenged traditional ideas about **SCULPTURE**.

By the end of the 1970s, Minimalism had triumphed in America and Europe, with Carl Andre, Dan Flavin, Donald Judd, and Sol LeWitt joining one of the movement's first artists, Frank Stella (page 117), as key innovators. Andre frequently used bricks or tiles for his sculptures; Flavin created works with fluorescent light bulbs bought from hardware stores; Judd had skilled workers build his shiny, colored squares and rectangles; Stella painted large, colorful stripes. The artists presented their paintings and sculptures on walls, in corners, or directly on the floor, making space and architecture important aspects of their works.

FRANK STELLA

1936–, United States of America

One of the most important
living American artists, known for his
colorful paintings and sculptures based on
geometric shapes and patterns

Frank Stella is an American artist, best known as a pioneer of the Minimalism movement. Stella showed great artistic talent at a young age. While at school, he realized that his true calling was to be an ABSTRACT painter, and he learned from the Abstract Expressionists (page 98) who came before him.

When he moved to New York City in the late 1950s, however, Stella reacted against their expressive use of paint and preferred "flatter" surfaces.

Stella focused on the basic elements of an artwork—color, shape, and **COMPOSITION**. He developed many paintings within the same series. He used acrylic paints in bright colors, arranged in straight or curved lines, within **GEOMETRICALLY** shaped canvases.

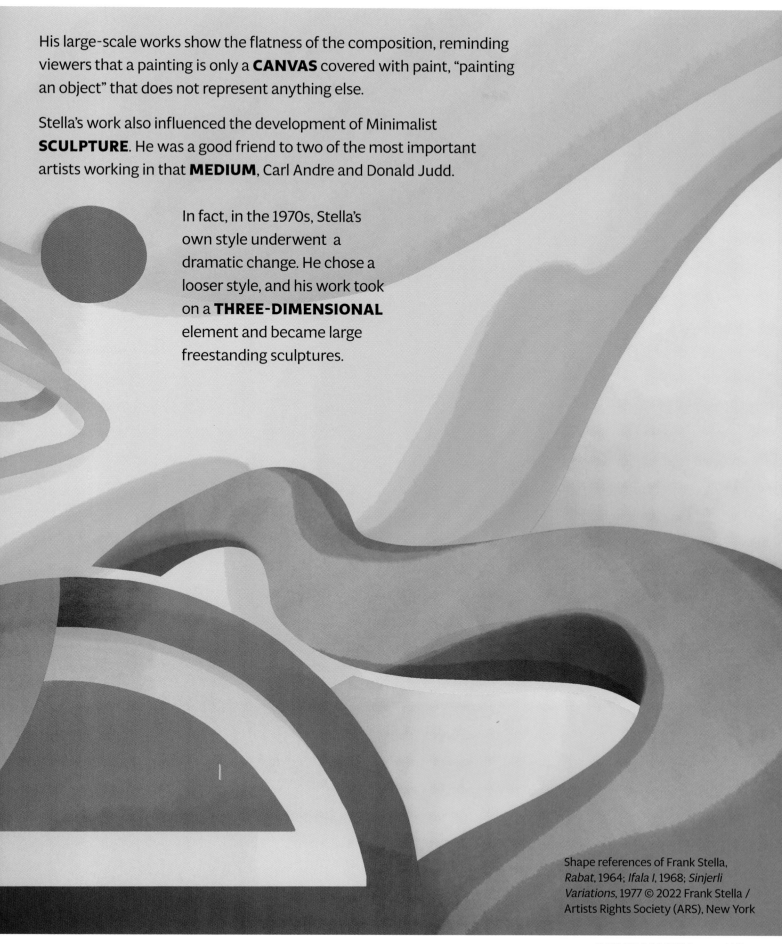

His large-scale works show the flatness of the composition, reminding viewers that a painting is only a **CANVAS** covered with paint, "painting an object" that does not represent anything else.

Stella's work also influenced the development of Minimalist **SCULPTURE**. He was a good friend to two of the most important artists working in that **MEDIUM**, Carl Andre and Donald Judd.

In fact, in the 1970s, Stella's own style underwent a dramatic change. He chose a looser style, and his work took on a **THREE-DIMENSIONAL** element and became large freestanding sculptures.

Shape references of Frank Stella, *Rabat*, 1964; *Ifala I*, 1968; *Sinjerli Variations*, 1977 © 2022 Frank Stella / Artists Rights Society (ARS), New York

RAINBOW STELLA

What you need:

tape

pencil

10 sheets thin
colored paper,
various colors

double-
sided tape

scissors

round-
shaped
objects

LET'S GET MESSY!

Step 1

Collect eight round-shaped objects, each a different size, each different by similar increments. Arrange these in order of size and match each size, except the largest one, with colored paper. Trace and cut out the seven circles on the colored paper.

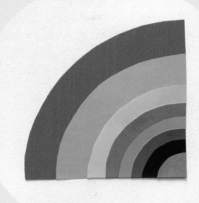

Step 2

Secure the circles on top of each other with double-sided tape. Cut the circles into quarters. Combine two of the quarters to make a square shape and leave the other two as quarters.

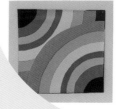

Step 3

Trace the largest circular object onto colored paper and cut it into quarters to make a border for your rainbow quarters. To make the square border, layer the combined square in step 2 onto a piece of colored paper and draw a border, then cut it out. Tape the rainbow shapes to their borders and mix and match them to create your composition!

GLOSSARY

Abstract - Art that does not represent real life, be it people, objects, or sceneries. Instead, Abstract artists use simplified marks, colors, and shapes.

Art movement - A group of artists making art of a similar style, or sharing similar beliefs at a given time.

Canvas - A surface used for painting or creating art on.

Collage - A technique and an art form using paper, newspaper, fabric, cloth, or other material that is cut up, arranged, and stuck down onto a surface.

Composition - The way a picture is arranged and how the different parts of the picture fit together.

Exhibition - A display of artworks shown to the public, usually held in a gallery or museum.

Gallery - A place where artists can show and sell their artworks, often as an exhibition.

Geometric - Shapes that are based on geometry, such as circles, ovals, rectangles, squares, and triangles.

Landscape - A genre of art depicting natural scenery, such as lakes, mountains, the sea, sky, and trees.

Manifesto - A written document or public statement that outlines the aims and intentions of a person or group.

Medium - The material used to make an artwork, such as clay, paints, paper, or pastels.

Mural - A large painting usually painted on a wall or ceiling.

Portraiture – A genre of art that represents a person where the face is always included. Sometimes, a portrait doesn't look like the person but still shows their likeness, personality, or even mood. A self-portrait is a painting that the artist makes of himself or herself.

Print – A method of transferring an image from one surface to another. Many copies can be made of the same image. Print types include engraving, lithography, screen print, and woodcut.

Sculpture – A three-dimensional artwork made by carving, casting, constructing, or modeling.

Sketch – A drawing that is done before the final painting.

Still life – A type of painting that shows an arrangement of nonmoving objects, such as flowers, fruits, plates, vases, and more.

Subject – What the artist has chosen to draw, paint, or represent.

Symbol – Something that represents another thing; for example, a book could represent knowledge and a butterfly could mean transformation.

Texture – How a painting looks or feels, rough or smooth; sometimes this can mean thicker paint or the use of different materials on the canvas.

Three-dimensional (3D) – Something that is not flat and that can be measured in three directions—depth, length, and width.

Acknowledgments

Writing a book is much harder than I thought and more rewarding than I could ever have imagined. None of this would have been possible without my husband and best friend, Nicholas. He was the one who believed in my crafty mess and inspired me to document my journey to share with others. Even at times when I wanted to give up, he remained steadfast in his support, seeing me through every struggle and all my successes. He was as important to finishing this book as I was.

I am also eternally grateful to my parents, who always supported me in my dreams and visions. They have taught me persistence, discipline, respect, and so much more that has shaped me and helped me succeed in life. More importantly, I feel every day their unconditional love and look up to them as my role models in life.

A very special thanks to my incredible illustrator, Shannon. You have become more than a collaborator, but a close friend. I deeply appreciate all the time, thought, and effort you have contributed toward making this project a reality. I am grateful for your agility and flexibility, as well as the continued energy and passion that you bring.

Writing a book about art history and kids crafts has been a surreal process, particularly witnessing the growth in interest in the subject in my own children over the past few years. I am indebted to Jonathan Simcosky at Quarry Books for believing in me, for his unwavering support, and for his ongoing commitment in advocating for this book. I am also grateful to all the editorial and design help at Quarto. It is because of their efforts and encouragement that I have a book to share, and to see it on the shelves of stores and libraries is something I would never have imagined in a million years.

About the Author

Stephanie Ho Poon is an art historian with a double master's degree from University of Cambridge and Sotheby's Institute of Art. She is a cultural professional who is passionate about education and crafting. She consults for major art institutions and organizations around the world and sits on the Advisory Council of Design Trust, the Advisory Committee of MILL6's Centre for Heritage, Arts, and Textiles, and serves as a board member of Ocean Park Corporation, chairing its Conservation and Education subcommittee. *Modern Art for Kids* is her debut children's book. Like many mothers, she strives to find a balance between her career and her family, and this book is the representation of combining her two life passions. She lives with her husband and three children in Hong Kong and regularly shares their crafting activities via Instagram @littlecitytales.

Index

Also Available

Art Lab for Kids
978-1-59253-765-5

Drawing Workshop for Kids
978-1-63159-943-9

Organic Artist for Kids
978-1-63159-767-1

Science Art and Drawing Games for Kids
978-0-7603-7216-6

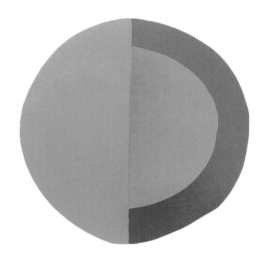